THE DOG NAMED
KANE

Editor: Mary Jane King— She is an experienced proofreader and editor.

Copyright © 2020 by Sarah Tuck

This is a work of a true story. Names, characters places and incidents are the product of the author's real-life story or are true events.

These names of one actual persons, living or dead were changed to protect the innocent and the events, or locale is entirely true.

All rights reserved. No part of this book may be reproduced or used in any manner without written permission of the copyright owner except for the use of quotations in a book review.

Sarah Tuck Book for children/9-14years and older Readers/Authorship:

Book Manufactured in United States of America

First Edition

Library of Congress in Publication Data
ISBN: 9780578792989 (paperback)
ISBN: 9780578792972 (e-book)

Table of Contents

CHAPTER 1 1

   INTRO : THE DOG NAMED KANE 1

CHAPTER 2 9

   KANE IS GROWING UP NOW 9

CHAPTER 3 18

   KANE LIKES OTHER ANIMALS 18

CHAPTER 4 24

   KANE HAS TURNED 5 MONTHS OLD 24

CHAPTER 5 29

   KANE'S STAY-AWAY FROM HOME 29

CHAPTER 6 36

   KANE REUNITES WITH HIS FAMILY 36

CHAPTER 7 40

   KANE'S NEW TOYS AND TREATS 40

AFTERWORD 45

ABOUT THE AUTHOR 46

CHAPTER 1

Intro

THE DOG NAMED KANE

The story you are about to read is a true story of a dog named Kane who was born on April, 27, 2020 in Munfordville, Kentucky where he once lived. He was brought to Franklin, Kentucky on June 8, 2020, by his owner Lauren who pledged to love and care for him while giving him a new home.

She had become the new mother of Kane, and his second owner Ronnell...was Kane's daddy...who pledged to love and care for him as well.

He was Lauren's doggy daddy. He was actually the one who introduced Kane to her.

Kane was a long way from home and the family he once knew was left back in Munfordville, Kentucky.

Now it was his time for him to venture out into new places and things.

As he grew and begin to notice the area, he started looking around; noticing things were a little different than what he had been used to back home.

He didn't know anyone in Franklin, Kentucky and he was new to the area.

But as time moved on he managed to make friends and had all kinds of love surrounding him each and every day.

Kane had a stunning look about himself.   He had a brown coat of fur with a tan splash on his face right between his eyes, around his nose and under his chin and belly.

He's eyes lighten up like shiny bars of gold.

He was the cutest dog you would have ever wanted to lay your eyes on.

Once you saw him you would have fallen in love with him. This is how adorable he was.

On Kane's first night in his new home...Ronnell had purchased a crate for him to sleep in. He adjusted to his new bed that night and slept like a little baby. And It didn't take him long to adjust to his new home.

The owner's mother didn't know about Kane yet. Until one day she was with Lauren and she pulled up at her girlfriend's house and Lauren asked her if she wanted to see the dog.

Granny Sarah was shocked to know that she had gone ahead and gotten a dog without her knowing about it. The last time the two of them had spoken about her getting a dog, Granny Sarah had replied no. And Lauren knew this.

Lauren had wanted a dog ever since she was a little girl. But Granny Sarah worked two jobs and wasn't able to help her take care of a dog.

This may have been one of the reasons she didn't get one before now.

She knew you had to put a lot of work in when taking care of a dog.

So, Granny Sarah was unaware of her going ahead in getting the dog.

But when she brought Kane out of the house and over to the car for her to see.   She immediately fell in love with him.

She knew Lauren was grown now and was making her own decisions.

And from what she could see…she felt she had made a good decision in getting Kane.

Granny Sarah had no trouble after that accepting Kane into her home and caring for him too.

This time came sooner than she had expected it too.

On the day of the fourth of July, Lauren was in a truck accident.

Her neck was troubling her and she was sorer from being jerked around.

She had to be off from work for three days.   And this is when Granny Sarah decided to let Kane come home with them.

Being together as a family was very important to Granny Sarah…and she knew this would make Lauren happy too.

So, she had his crate moved over to her home where he would have his own bed to sleep in. Then she was able to take care of the both of them. And from then own Kane was the center of their lives. The days passed by and Granny Sarah and Kane had begun to bond together into a close relationship while Lauren was getting well.

Kane was once again getting used to staying in a different place.

And it didn't take him long to win Granny Sarah over to his side.

She loved to see him running through the house and playing with his toys.

He would even walk across the floor and run up to her wagging his tail with his pink tongue hanging out wanting her to pick him up.

Once you would pick him up and loved on him he was satisfied for a while...until he wanted to get down and get into something else.

Then he would go and play with his toys and chew on everything he could put into his mouth.

Since he was little and cute they laughed at him and let him kind of have his way on the first.

That was until...he started getting bigger and he was chewing on the rugs, papers, socks and all kinds of things.

It wasn't funny anymore...because he was becoming a pest in destroying things.

When Lauren's mother told her what he had done when she came home one day from work. Lauren said, "Kane is going to have to get a job."

They both laughed and looked at him from the side of their face with their eye.

He was shut up in his cage at this very moment looking out between the crate wondering what was going on with these two.

He knew he was in trouble. He looked so innocent looking through the cage...you couldn't help but to feel sorry for him.

Time after time he was warned about chewing on the things that wasn't his toys.

So one day they brought him some more toys for him to play with hoping he would ignore the rugs and all kind of stuff.

But this didn't do any good, he would still continue chewing on the rugs and all kind of stuff from time to time. I'm sure he thought these things looked better and tasted better than his toys.

And, this was only half of the problems Lauren was having with Kane. He was still confused on where he needed to use the bathroom.

He would be playing in the house, and all of a sudden he would stop and just go right in the middle of the floor.

This really upset Granny Sarah, and Lauren too.

She had been instructed prior to him coming to put his face in it and use a newspaper by giving him a few licks to warn him not to do this again. This was a way of teaching him not to go on the rug in the house. He was to wait until he went outside to use the bathroom.

While he was being trained a few months down the road. Kane had become aware of where he was to use the bathroom.

After several attempts of training him, he had become a pro in knowing where to go.

He had learned to bark to let you know he had to go outside or he would walk over to the door and stand in front of it and look at it.

By this time he was on his way of getting smarter and he was receiving more treats than ever now.

On July 22, 2020, Lauren had text Granny Sarah at 7:10 am, asking her to take Kane to the Veterinarian for his shots. His appointment was at 10:30 a.m. and she wanted to know if she could take him.

She replied, "Yes, I can."

Lauren then texted her and said, "He's got to be there at 10:30 mama, and there will be a sign out front with their phone number on it. You will call them when you pull up and tell them that you are outside. They will come out and get him."

Granny Sarah said, "Alright, I will get up so I can get ready to take him."

Once she got there she thought that he was to be at one place and he was scheduled at another place. But Granny Sarah acted like she knew where to go.

She called Lauren and she called the clinic and said she's on her way with Kane. Once she arrived she called...inside and the doctor came out and took Kane from the car after she asked Granny Sarah some questions, and took him inside.

While Kane was at his doctor's visit, Granny Sarah had time to run over to the store to pick him up some treats for Kane.

When she came back within five minutes, she got a call saying they would be bringing Kane back out to the car. But first, they were needing for her to pay his bill.

Granny Sarah asked, "How much is it?"

The lady said, "It will be sixty-six dollars and sixty cents."

Granny Sarah didn't know that she was going to have to pay for the visit too. So, she reached in her purse and pulled out her master card, and paid for Kane's doctor visit.

Later on, one of the assistant came out to the car with Kane and said, "He's doing good, he has no worms, he weighs 21.8 pounds and his next appointment will be on August 12, 2020, at 10:30 in the morning."

Then she called Lauren and updated her on how the visit went and told her, "You owe me sixty-six dollars and sixty cents."

Lauren laughed and said, "Alright, mama I'm going to send it to you through the cash app right now."

You see Granny Sarah didn't mind doing for Kane but, she didn't want to take on too much of his responsibilities. This could be another reason why Lauren didn't get this dog when she was younger.

Granny Sarah had a lot planned for Kane but this was not one of the plans.

When Granny Sarah got him home she gave him some Tylenol to keep him from running a fever and getting sick.

But this didn't help. At about 6:30, he started getting sick and vomiting and looking so pitiful.

Granny Sarah wasn't feeling fine about Kane being sick, I think she was getting sick too. This is how much they had become attached to each other.

Lauren happened to be there and called her friend Carrie to reassure Granny Sarah that everything was going to be alright with Kane.

Carrie said, "This is normal Miss Sarah, I promise you he will be fine."

He laid down in his crate and went to sleep. Then later, he got up and started playing with his toys as if nothing had happened.

The next day he was up and ready to start another day with Granny Sarah. She decided to take him with her riding in her van to the park and other places. He loved to go riding with her.

She would let him look out the window so he could see all the exciting things while she was driving.

Soon after that, Granny Sarah had realized that she had made a big mistake by taking him riding in the van.

Each time she grabbed her keys to leave the house, he would whine and bark to go riding with her in the van.

He had been watching her and Lauren long enough to know when they were going to be leaving without taking him.

These were the signs that would alert him when they were going somewhere.

When they would pick up the keys, he could hear them jingle, seeing them change their clothes, and then stoop down to tie their shoes.

Kane was beginning to catch on to things that they didn't even think he was paying attention to.

This is when she knew she had started something she would have to keep up with him for a very long time.

So, on a special occasion, Granny Sarah would take time out to take him with her riding in the van.

She would take him out for walks around 6:30 or 7:00 a.m. in the mornings and making sure he would potty before coming back into the house.

She would also sit outside and watch him play while she was enjoying being outdoors. These two were becoming an item in spending time together.

And as they were becoming an item, Granny Sarah could see that Lauren was getting a little jealous of her and Kane spending so much time together.

Why? You might be asking, this was because at night Granny Sarah would say, "Goodnight Kane."

Then as she was walking out of the room Lauren would say, "Goodnight mama."

Granny Sarah would laugh and say, "Goodnight Lauren."

This is how she could tell that Lauren was beginning to feel left out of the circle.

So, from that day forward, she made sure she would always say, "Goodnight to the both of them."

This way, Lauren would never feel left out of the circle.

Granny Sarah loved the both of them and she was glad that Kane had come to join them in their home.

CHAPTER 2

KANE IS GROWING UP NOW

In this chapter, you will see how much Kane has grown, how bigger he is and what a big dog he has become.

His owners have been watching Kane while he has been growing; since he's been in their care.

Lauren and Ronnell have been discussing how much larger he has become.

So, Ronnell decided to go out and purchase a larger crate for him to stay in.

And I'm sure Kane was glad to be getting a new crate too.

Kane was beginning to stand tall now on his two back legs. And on July 27, 2020, he was outside looking out into the streets and around the yard.

Letting the neighbors know that he was on guard duty now of watching out for his Granny Sarah and his owner Lauren.

If anybody stepped foot in this yard... they were going to have to deal with him.

He let everybody know that passed by on that street to know that he was the king up in their place.

And he was glad to be letting everyone know it.

He would always sit close to his Granny Sarah and lay his head on her lap whenever he had the chance to. When he would do this...she would always pat and rub him telling him he was granny's baby.

She loved him and he loved her too.

Kane made this very clear the day the plumber came to fix the pipe that was clogged.

He sat by her the whole time he was there and he barked at him to let him know he was there to guard his granny.

Granny Sarah reassured Kane that everything was going to be alright and then he stopped barking and sat still.

He would watch the plumber closely as he entered in and out of the house.

Making sure that the plumber didn't bother Granny Sarah.

This pleased Granny Sarah to know that Kane loved her so much that he was on guard the whole time making sure she would be alright.

Then the plumber finished, she paid him and he left.

Later when the plumber had left, she gave him some treats for being such a good guard dog.

He was eating those bacon strips like they were going out of style.

Then he started playing with his toys.

As the day went by he was getting tired, so he decided to go inside his crate to get comfortable by laying on his back and took a nap.

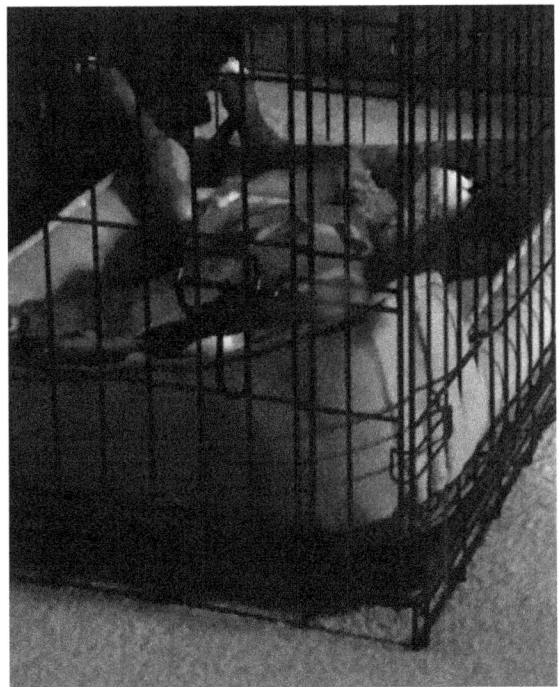

He was well relaxed and was glad to get him some rest after being on guard duty for Granny Sarah.

As she was watching him sleeping in his crate she decided to snap a picture of him.

He looked so cute lying there on his back with his legs up in the air.

Then she text the picture to Lauren and told her what happened.

Lauren laughed and was happy to know that he was looking out for her mama.

Lauren then FaceTime her mother and said, "I have something to show you…are you watching?"

She said, "Yes, what is it?"

Lauren then showed her another dog that she had with her.

Granny Sarah was frantic about what she had just seen.

Why she couldn't believe that Lauren had gone and gotten another dog and they were still trying to train Kane and keep him under control.

Granny Sarah said, "We can't take on another dog right now. Kane is all that we can handle right now."

Lauren laughed and said, "Calm down mama, he is the neighbor's dog. I'm just keeping him for a little while that's all."

Granny Sarah took a deep breath and said, "Thank God." She was wondering how she was going to help her with another dog.

Lauren said, "But I figured Kane needed a playmate to keep him company."

Granny Sarah said, "Well he has enough family to keep him company."

Lauren laughed and said, "Well I have to get back to work."

Granny Sarah said, "Alright, I will talk to you later."

Since Kane had become part of the family now Granny Sarah would take him around some of the other family members. She would make sure they all knew who Kane was. He barked at them the first time, but when she explained to him that they were family and these were your cousin, aunt, and friends.

He calmed down and showed them love, by trying to go with them and licking on their faces and hands. This is how he would bond with you.

Soon it was time for Kane to go over to his friend's house to play.

His friend's name was Zoey, she was a little older than Kane. But they played well together.

And not to mention Zoey's owner was one of Lauren best friends.

These dogs would run around in this big fenced-in backyard and have the best time of their lives.

It must have been love at first sight...because these two were becoming quite chummy.

The reason why Granny Sarah had this thought was because there was another picture that had surfaced and they looked to be doing more than just playing.

It looks like Zoey was trying to sneak in a kiss on Kane.

This would explain why Kane was so eager to go over to Zoey's house to play.

It seemed like he had a crush on her.

Or maybe this picture looked like they were trying to kiss.

Or maybe they both were thirsty for water with their tongues hanging out. You know looks can be deceiving.

"But you didn't hear this from me," said Granny Sarah under her voice.

Anyway, she was glad that Kane and Zoey had a good friendship and he had found someone who could understand him in his language.

This away he didn't feel like he was all alone...even though he had a lot of people who loved and cared for him.

By now Kane had different individuals coming up to his owner asking is this Kane? And she would answer yes.

The little boy named Troy was with his friend and said, "His name is Kane and I know him."

Kane was beginning to be popular now.

Soon afterwards, it was time for Kane to go back home and leave Zoey.

When Kane went home he was so tired from running and playing a lot with Zoey while he was over to her house.

So, when he went to sleep...Granny Sarah decided to take another picture of him sleeping while he was lying in his bed.

He always looked so precious...there wasn't enough words to express how he looked.

Granny Sarah knew he was tired from the way he was snoring and she filmed him snoring as well.

She had heard him snore before, but it was nothing like the snoring he was doing on this day.

She enjoyed having him lay beside her by her bed while she was watching television.

He was a sight for sore eyes to see.

Before he went to sleep, she caught him watching television for a few minutes.

He was learning to pick up on different things as he was growing up.

You could tell he was spoiled and I'm sure Granny Sarah had a lot to do with him being spoiled.

On September 8, 2020, Kane was going for his second grooming visit to have his toenails trimmed.

Carrie, Lauren's friend...was coming to get him to take him to have it done.

She would ask to take him with her when she would have to take Zoey to have hers done.

This would help Lauren out because she was busy trying to hold down two jobs to help pay for some of the things Kane needed in taking care of his personal needs.

And Ronnell would take care of the rest of them.

Kane was getting bigger and was learning more about being disciplined.

Lauren and Granny Sarah decided to let him attend their parking lot service on one Sunday morning in September, 2020.

Yes, they would have the service in their cars due to the coronavirus.

This was to help keep everyone safe while they were having church.

Kane was good at first but then he wouldn't be still...he wanted to get up front with them and lick on them. This was because he felt like he was being left out.

Being in the back seat by himself...he was beginning to feel lonely.

He was barking and didn't want to play anymore with his toys that they had brought with them for him to play with.

This is when they decided he wouldn't be able to attend church with them too many more times.

Not unless they could think of a better plan.

When they got home with him, he was able to run and jump into Granny Sarah's lap for her to pat and rub on him once again.

He was happy now he had their attention. Being the center of attention made him so happy.

How you could always tell...he would wag his tail, jump up and down, and with excitement, and he would take off running through the house as fast as he could.

He was running so fast you would have thought he was at a dog race or something.

This is why they had to put him back into his crate from time to time, and they taught him not to run in the house by saying no and stop.

He soon learned that he was to wait until he went outside to run and play.

CHAPTER 3

KANE LIKES OTHER ANIMALS

Kane was beginning to see and be around other animals. He likes looking and watching other animals on the television, outdoors and in pictures.

Here is one of the pictures of a pair of zebras he was shown.

He just looked at them as if he knew them.

And when the animals would come close to him he would sniff them.

Especially, when he was around other dogs.

I'm sure it amazes him to see other animals due to his nature of being one himself.

It's probably a sense of nature that takes his mind back to being an animal too...that helps him relate to them.

He even had a chance to see a picture of some camels.

He stood there wagging his tail with excitement as if he knew what was going on.

Even though Kane is lovable and sweet sometimes, he also has a wild streak, a side of himself you wouldn't believe.

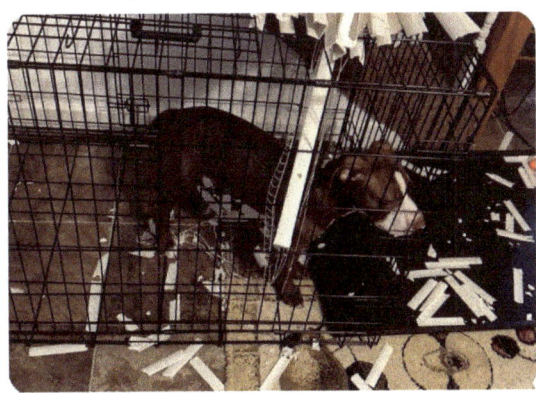

Here is an example of him being naughty. He tore up some blinds one day and he was barking when Lauren entered into the house to see about him because he knew he was in trouble.

Lauren shook her head took a picture and said, "I was told to get a pit bull they are friendly animals they say."

But now she was beginning to wonder if she had made a mistake or not.

She cleaned up the mess, had a talk with him, and gave him a pass this time.

Boy, he was lucky she didn't give him a spanking.

Maybe because it was kind of her fault for leaving the blinds so close to him.

Anyway, overall...she loves Kane and he is fortunate to have an owner like Lauren and Granny Sarah.

You can't help but to feel sorry for him...due to he was taken from his family and now he's had to make a new one.

But this wasn't the only thing Kane had done.

He had watched Lauren on this particular day sitting in the living room eating a bowl of cereal.

He had waited on that day until Lauren went into the bathroom to use it. Knowing, that she had left the remaining of some cereal and milk in the bowl on the coffee table from earlier that day.

He walked over and decided to help himself to what was left.

And when she came back from the bathroom...there he stood on his back two legs with her bowl of cereal between his two paws. Eating her cereal until it was all gone.

She just shook her head and laughed at him.

I feel like this is the reason he gets so many breaks. But, you have to let him know who is the boss, or he will take over and have you sitting outside.

Here's another one of his precious pictures of him looking outside through the blinds in the living room while Lauren was working.

She just happens to notice him looking out the window on that day when she said, "He is meddling with the neighbors next door."

Then she took a picture and sent it to her mama, Granny Sarah.

Granny Sarah said, "Aw, he just wants to get outside and play."

Lauren laughed and said, "No, the neighbors are outside and he is meddling with them."

Granny Sarah laughed and at that very moment, she had started to

realize that her little grandbaby Kane was now growing up.

He was standing taller than ever in this picture. He had grown almost twice his size, it looked like more than he was in the picture in the beginning of this book.

Granny Sarah knew he wouldn't stay small forever...but she was overwhelmed in how big he was getting in such a short length of time that he had been with them.

Once again Kane had touched Granny Sarah's heart and she loved him even more than before.

On September 25, 2020, Granny Sarah decided to take another picture of Kane playing in the floor with his ball that he had almost ruined.

He had been to the groomer awhile ago to have his toenails clipped. But in this picture, it looks like he is up for another visit very soon.

He would make you laugh at him in how he would lay his back legs on the floor and sprawled out to play.

There was never a dull moment when Kane was around.

Kane has a unique way of playing and making you laugh.

He would place his paws over something he wasn't supposed to have when you would get on him about it...looking around as if to say who are you talking to...me?

This left Granny Sarah speechless.

She was tickled in seeing all the funny things Kane were doing now.

There was one time he impressed Granny Sarah when she was having problems with her knee.

She was sitting in the chair rubbing her knee complaining when Kane walked over to her, jumped up, and placed his paws on her knee to keep it from hurting her.

This is when Granny Sarah realized he had a human side…in being compassionate to others.

She was overwhelmed with joy and happiness to know Kane knew how to even show her this side of him.

They had become closer and closer over the period he was there in her home.

CHAPTER 4

KANE HAS TURNED 5 MONTHS OLD

Here you will see how much bigger and taller Kane has growned into being the King of the place at his new home.

On October 2, 2020, Granny Sarah had taken Kane outside to play for a while...when she notice he stopped and stood straight up on his two back legs looking around checking and scoping the area out.

He would look from side to side watching and listening to hear what he was seeing to make sure there was no danger. Watching him...gave Granny Sarah a sense of protection, even more, to know that he was being alert and so protective even more now.

Kane saw some of the neighbors walking down the street with their children. He looked from side to side then he stood up and started sniffing and trying to smell the scent that was in the air.

He was being very observant of what was going on around him.

While taking in their scent to make sure if he seen them before and smelled their scent so that he would be familiar with them.

Sometimes, when they would go outside Granny Sarah wouldn't put his collar on him and he would wander out into the street to greet the neighbors who were out walking.

They would actually stop and rub him and talk to him while he was standing there wagging his tail waiting to get some love from them.

This made Granny Sarah wonder if he was going to be able to handle the difference between someone trying to hurt him by him being so friendly to everyone.

Until a few days later, when Granny Sarah was going outside with Kane to take him to the park.

While she was trying to lock the front door she heard a voice say no.

When she took a look...Kane was standing right in front of another dog and the owner that lived across the street.

The neighbor was trying to get her leash on the harness of her dog and was trying to hold him at the same time.

Granny Sarah ran and grabbed Kane harness and said, "I'm sorry I didn't know that you were out here. We were on our way out so I let him out first then I was going to lock the door."

She was apologizing for her dog running over in their yard, but Kane wasn't having it. He was barking and lunging toward the little dog while Granny Sarah was trying to pull him back.

Basically, letting him know you have crossed the line now you are over in my yard and I've got to protect me and Granny Sarah.

Granny Sarah had to pull and wrestle with Kane to put him in the van.

She was never so glad to shut the door on him to know that he was safe and so was the neighbor and her dog.

This is when she found out that he would be there for them when he needed to be there. Kane wasn't playing that day.

He had shown his strength and his ability of his duty of being on guard when he needed to be. Without a doubt, he was not slow or sleeping on his job this time.

Then she got into the van, cranked it, and proceeded to the park.

While Granny Sarah was driving to the park...she was telling Kane how proud she was to see he had stepped up in guarding them and then she stopped at a nice area for them to get out.

When they got out of the van, Kane was so eager to run and play and started sniffing the area.

Soon afterwards when he was still, he saw a lady fishing down by the water at the park.

He soon started staring, growling, and barking at her.

Granny Sarah tried to explain to Kane that it was ok and she was only fishing and everything is going to be alright.

Finally she opened the side door on the van, took her seat, and started to watch the lady fishing.

While she was watching her, she happened to look down and she seen that Kane had taken a seat right beside her still with his eyes on the lady down by the water.

Then he jumped up in the van still watching the lady, then he stood still, and sat down again on his two back legs right beside Granny Sarah.

He wasn't going to take his eyes off the lady, nor was he going to let anything happen to Granny Sarah.

This is how protective he was over her.

Later she closed the door and then they walked around in the park and had the best time of their lives.

Kane was even running and jumping…he was having so much fun.

Then it was time to head home when Granny Sarah opened the side door on the van…to let Kane in and then shut the door. She walked

over to the driver's side and got inside, shut the door, and then she drove off.

Once they got home, she parked the van, got out, and then went over to the passenger side and let Kane out. Then they went into the house.

She poured some water in the bowl for Kane to drink and put some dog food in his pan.

He ate his food and took some sips of water till he was finish and then he went into the living room to play with his toys.

Granny Sarah turned on the television and took her seat to relax.

While she was watching television, she looked over at Kane and he had fallen asleep. He was so tired from running and playing in the park.

This is how Granny Sarah knew that he had enjoyed himself by being at the park.

CHAPTER 5

KANE'S STAY-AWAY FROM HOME

On Wednesday night October 7, 2020, Kane was taken to Carrie's house to stay and play with Zoey while Lauren, his owner, took her trip to California to celebrate her birthday for a few days.

But before Kane left, Granny Sarah hugged and rubbed him to let him know that she was going to miss him and told him to be good while he was gone.

She hated to see him leave her, but she wasn't able to take care of him.

Lauren would have left him with Granny Sarah to take care of him, but she wasn't feeling well.

She had been to the doctor on that day and had to have a flu shot and have her yearly lab work done.

When she came home from the doctor, she didn't feel well.

She started coughing, nose running and sneezing as if she had a cold.

Granny Sarah didn't want Kane to get sick too.

Nor was she capable of seeing to him, to make sure he would be alright.

So, Lauren made the decision on taking him to her friend's house.

On the next morning around 6:45, Lauren left to travel to Nashville, Tennessee to board the plane for her trip to California.

She landed safely in California and contacted Granny Sarah to let her know she had made it there alright around 1:19 p.m.

Since they both had left the house, it was so quiet and Granny Sarah realized she was there at home all by herself and this is when she

began to cry because she felt so lonely now that they were not there to keep her company.

She had been so busy doing for them and making sure they were taken care of. She had forgotten how much she needed them to help her through times like these.

But her loneliness didn't last two long because Granny Sarah was an unique person with strong capabilities of making things happen to help keep her mind occupied in times like these.

She pulled it together…and within a couple of days, she had started back writing and thinking on her book that she was writing. She couldn't wait to finish writing it so she could get it published.

Telling the world about her grandbaby's dog named Kane.

She was excited and anxious about seeing Kane on the front cover of one of her amazing books.

Meanwhile, she had asked Carrie, Lauren's friend, if she could have some pictures to see what all Kane had been up to while he was staying at her house.

While she was waiting on her to send her the pictures to see what all he had been up to, she was thinking about how tired he might be from all that running and playing he was doing over there. Due to the fact that every time Kane came home from having so much fun with Zoey,

he would wind up sleeping for at least two days just to catch up on his rest.

And his nose would sometimes be red from where they had been biting each other. This is just the way they would play with each other.

When the pictures came through the phone, Granny Sarah was tickled with what she was seeing.

"Look-a-there, he is asleep on the floor," she said to herself.

She had already pictured him

being tired from all that playing he had been doing.

And this picture had only confirmed what she had been thinking.

Seeing him in this picture made her miss him even more. And I'm sure he was missing her just as much.

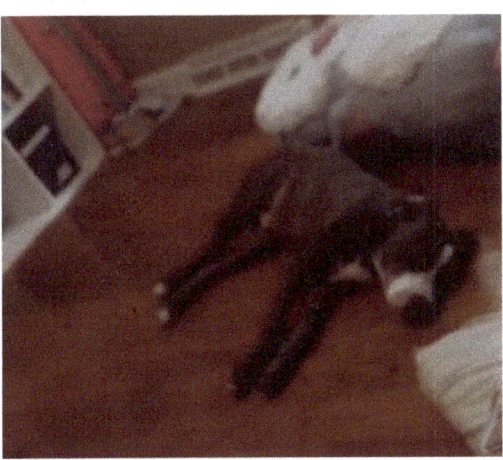

Even the next picture was showing her he was still tired and worn out from running and playing so much over there.

He still had to take another nap to be able to get his energy back to keep up with Zoey.

Granny Sarah was glad that he was having fun, but this still didn't change the fact that she was missing him and wanted him to come home to be with her.

Meanwhile, she had gotten a picture from Lauren, her daughter, and the owner of Kane...showing her she was having an awesome time.

And this picture did show how much of a great time she was having on her vacation.

There she was at the top of the mountain enjoying herself.

She deserved it though...because she worked two jobs to help take care of Kane buying him toys, treats, dog food, getting his toenails trimmed and she takes him to the veterinarian to make sure he's up on his shots.

And Ronnell, her baby dog's daddy, still helps take care of the other half of these things.

Plus Lauren looks out for her mama when she can to make sure she has everything she needs.

She has been a beautiful gift to her mama since Lauren's father passed away when she was at the age of four.

His death has made them grow closer together through the years...and

they have always have been there for each other...in making sure they had each other's back.

This is why Kane is lucky...and has an awesome owner because she knows what it's like to be the only child left behind.

When she saw him she wanted to give him a home and the love he would remember for the rest of his life.

This was the first time they have ever been apart this long since she brought him to his new home.

Sometimes, we all need a break every once and a while to be with our friends and do some of the things we have on our bucket list to do.

Because tomorrow isn't promised to anyone...and we should live life to the fullest that is given to us.

As we become older in life we begin to realize these things.

So, this was one of the things on Lauren's bucket list she wanted to do.

Lauren did check on Kane because she was missing him as much as Granny Sarah was.

She had even called and chatted with Ronnell on how much she missed him and he reassured her that Kane was fine.

But until she gets back to see him, she is going to continue enjoying her vacation.

And I'm sure Kane is enjoying playing with Zoey while his owner is away on vacation celebrating her birthday.

I'm sure Kane will be happy to see her when she gets home.

Standing there wagging his tail anxious for her to pick him up and give him some love...if he doesn't jump up on her first.

He has a bad habit of running up to her and jumping up on her and Granny Sarah when he sees them. It's because he missed being near them when they are out of his sight.

And he gets excited when he sees them again.

CHAPTER 6

KANE REUNITES WITH HIS FAMILY

As the time has went by, and on October 12, 2020, at 8:05 p.m. Lauren and Kane arrived at home. Granny Sarah was never so glad to see her when she came through the door.

They greeted each other and then Lauren took her bags to her room and laid down.

About 45 minutes later Ronnell had brought Kane home to see Lauren and Granny Sarah.

Lauren got out of the bed, came into the living room to see Kane. You could see he was glad to see her and she was glad to see him too.

Granny Sarah was sitting at the kitchen table, but she could see Kane when he walked in and stopped, and was looked at Granny Sarah bedroom door…and it was closed.

So, he turned and walked down the hallway toward the guest bedroom…and this door was closed too.

He then started walking back and forth behind the couch…thinking where was my Granny Sarah. His owner looked over at her mama and said, "You are not going to call him."

She shook her head and softly said, "No, he will find me."

Then Lauren looked down at Kane and asked, him, "What's wrong Kane?"

Granny Sarah spoke up again but this time a little louder and said, "I think he's looking for me."

Once he heard her voice he ran into the kitchen jumped up in her lap with his tail wagging glad to see his Granny Sarah.

Not only was his tail wiggling but his tongue was hanging out... he was so full of excitement.

She was so glad to see him just as much as he was glad to see her too.   Lauren just laughed and said, "Aw".

Once again the family was reunited and Granny Sarah wouldn't have to spend the night alone.

Granny Sarah rubbed and loved Kane as she was looking at him telling him how much bigger he had gotten than he was when he had left her.

After they spent some time together, Kane went into the living room to play with his toys.

When suddenly she looked around...and it wasn't fifteen minutes later she saw him lying on the floor past out asleep.

She could tell Kane was tired from the way he looked out of his eyes...and not to mention he was moving rather slow through the house.

Again she couldn't wait to take a picture of him lying on the floor looking adorable beside the rug he had been chewing on.

This look had made her day and not to mention to have her baby girl and Kane both home once again.

Granny Sarah was thanking God for blessing the both of them to come back home to her safely.

Then Granny Sarah continued on the computer writing her book on the story about Kane.

He would come up close to her and peep around the computer as if to say what are you doing granny?

This was the cutest sight you would have ever wanted to see.

An hour and half had passed by now when she noticed that Kane had awaken to try to play with his toys once again.

He could barely move the bone around...because he was still tired from all the playing and running he had done while he was over to Zoey's house.

He tried his best to play with some of his other toys...but soon he was out again for a while.

Then he woke up and walked over to Granny Sarah for her to hold him and she did. Then she took another picture of him.

Sitting there watching him...gave her a heartfelt moment of having him home for her to help take care of him once again.

She also noticed that it was time for him to go back to the groomer to have his toenails trimmed again.

Especially when he jumped up in her lap...she could feel the sharpness in her leg from his toenails.

In this picture, you could see the puffiness...around his eyes as he continued to stare at Granny Sarah while she was taking his picture.

You could see that he hadn't had a lot of rest.

He walked around the living room, and flopped down and sighed.

He seemed restless and acted as if he couldn't make up his mind to go sleep or play.

He would walk in and out of his crate trying to make his mind up about what he wanted to do.

Then finally Granny Sarah looked around and he was sleep again...this time he was in his crate.

She added this to the story, and then she cut off the computer, got up turned the light off, then she went to bed.

You can be sure that on this night Granny Sarah, Kane, and Lauren was all going to sleep like babies.

And Granny Sarah didn't have to feel all alone anymore.

CHAPTER 7

KANE'S NEW TOYS AND TREATS

On the next morning when Granny Sarah got up she went into the living room to see Kane. He was glad to see her too, he walked over to her slower than usual.

He was dragging his feet and she could tell he was still tired.

He jumped up on her and greeted her as usual, then she gave him some love by hugging and rubbing him.

She told him she had to go out to run some errands for about three hours.

Then she would be back to take him outside when she came back.

She hated to leave Kane since he had just come home.

But she had to leave him to take care of her business, then she told him that she would be back soon.

Then he walked over to Granny Sarah and laid on her lap.

He was showing her how glad he was to be back home with her and Lauren.

They had a great time together and then they went back inside the house and he started following Granny Sarah around from room to room.

Until she went and sat down in the living room to watch the television... while Kane was on the floor playing with his toys.

Then suddenly, he happens to hear a door slam then he jumped up and starred at the door until Lauren came up to the door unlocked it, and then she walked in.

He ran to her wagging his tail with excitement to see her. Then he started following Lauren from room to room sniffing on her.

Kane would have you laughing because he was so funny at times.

Especially, when Lauren or Granny Sarah would be at the kitchen table eating.

He would sit down on his back two legs and look up at them while they were eating hoping they would give him some of what they were having.

This would make Granny Sarah feel so sorry for Kane because he wasn't supposed to eat table food. Lauren wanted him to eat his dog food.

But Granny Sarah would give him pieces of bread and some potato chips from time to time…not to mention the chicken mini's he would get from Chick-fil-A.

Lauren was in on this though…every now and then. This is how they would treat him when they had to leave him for a while.

He loved getting treats to eat.

And when he was good he would get a lot of them.

When they ask him to sit, he would sit as straight as he could on his back two legs and looked up at you waiting for his treats.

If he was in his crate and wanted out of it…and you wouldn't let him out, he would turn his back on you, flop down in the crate, and pout.

This would tickle them in how much he would act like a little kid.

And most of all, he was spoiled from getting all the attention they had been giving him.

So, if he couldn't get their attention he would whine and move around in his crate looking at them…as if to say, "Why are you doing this to me?"

Oh, and don't let him turn his head from side to side when you asked him to stop doing that.

Making out like he didn't understand that you were talking to him.

This is when Granny Sarah would give in to him some of the times and be a little partial to him.

This was because she felt sorry for him.

But when she wanted him to mind her, she learned to be firm with him and make him mind her.

He didn't always like it but he started listening to her...and doing what she would ask him to do most of the time.

And when he wouldn't, she would make him get back into his crate, think about it, then she would let him back out again. This had begun to work too.

You could tell that he had started being cautious in what he was doing.

It was getting late, and it was time for them to go to bed, when Lauren decided to let Kane sleep in her room with her on this night.

They went into her room and cut off the light and then he laid down on the floor right beside her bed and went to sleep. He didn't roam around in the house either.

He was able to stay in her room until the next morning.

This was due to the fact he wasn't roaming all over the house at night and chewing on everything he could get a hold of.

You could tell that Kane was getting older and smarter in what his role was...in being on his best behavior to be able to stay out of his crate.

I guess you could say that he had graduated to another level to achieve this privilege.

On Wednesday morning October 14, 2020, Granny Sarah decided while she was out shopping...to pick Kane up some toys and a bag of treats.

When she came back home, she let Kane out of the crate and took him outside as she had promised him.   She let him relieved himself first.

Then afterwards, she opened the bag of treats and laid them aside. She then took the wheel on the strings and threw it into the yard trying to get Kane to bring it back to her.

But instead, he just flopped down and started chewing on it.

Later on, as she reached to pick up the treat to offer him for bringing it to her...he ran over to her to get the treat, but he didn't bring the wheel to her..

After several attempts, she decided to give it a rest.

This is when she realized she wasn't going to make a lot of progress on the first day.

So, after a while, she decided to go inside and try this again on another day.

Kane went into the kitchen to get some sips of water, then he came back into the living room and started playing with his toys.

Even though Kane has accomplished a lot since he's been there with his new family...he still has room to learn more and more as time goes on.

AFTERWORD

This story was a true story about a dog named Kane who was united with the daughter of the author of this book, whose name is Lauren. The author, Ms. Sarah Tuck, has always wanted to write a younger children's book after she wrote the one called Ray Jay's Senior Year. She wrote that book for the middle-school and high-school children, ages between thirteen through nineteen years of age. Not to mention the college children as well. Hoping they could see the different trials and tribulations that some of the other children their ages have to deal with and the parents too. Her goal was to also encourage the older kids to think before leaping out into the adult world while taking on more responsibilities. And now she wanted to share the joy of raising a baby puppy into an adult dog. While watching Kane go through the different changes in becoming an adult dog, she has learned to understand dogs and appreciate them more than she has in the past. By doing this, not only has she become Granny Sarah, but she has made a friend with Kane. A friend that she has learned will be there for her when she needs him to protect, love, and keep her from being lonely too. He has been the love of the both of these ladies' lives...and they will always cherish having him till death do them part.

ABOUT THE AUTHOR

Contact Information

Email: tuckproductions@yahoo.com

Facebook.com/protecting 2014

Twitter.com/sarah1057rabbit

Instagram.com/sarah_tuck_production2014

www.ingramcontent.com/pod-product-compliance
Lightning Source LLC
Chambersburg PA
CBHW062028290426
44108CB00025B/2830